M000217880

My Green Notebook

Notebook

"Know Thyself" Before Changing Jobs

A guided reflection to help you lead
with the best version of yourself

JOE BYERLY
AND
CASSIE CROSBY

Fulton Books, Inc.
Meadville, PA

Published by Fulton Books 2021

ISBN 978-1-63985-712-8 (paperback)
ISBN 978-1-63860-085-5 (hardcover)
ISBN 978-1-63860-084-8 (digital)

Printed in the United States of America

Foreword

I t's my honor to write the foreword to this reflective notebook. I'm sure it will help leaders in the military, and indeed many others, to evaluate their own thoughts and actions more carefully and more effectively. Achieving insight in this way cannot only improve your performance in a specific role but, more importantly, it can transform your character in general.

My area of expertise is ancient Stoic philosophy and its relationship with modern psychology, especially cognitive-behavioral therapy (CBT) and emotional-resilience training. Books like this build on an ancient tradition that goes back to Greece and Rome. Many people are unaware that the most famous Stoic teacher of all, Epictetus, wrote nothing. His words were transcribed and edited by a senior Roman general called Arrian of Nicomedia, who served as the military governor of Cappadocia (modern-day Turkey) under Emperor Hadrian. As well as being an avid student of Stoic philosophy and a highly-accomplished Roman statesman, Arrian was a prolific writer and an expert on cavalry training and tactics.

He describes Epictetus teaching a specific daily routine to his students (*Discourses* 4.6). Each morning they were to prepare for the day ahead by asking themselves what they need to do in order to further master their own fears and unruly desires and free themselves from any traces of unwarranted distress. They are to ask themselves what steps they must take to fulfill their potential for living wisely and in accord with virtues such as justice, courage, and temperance. Each evening they were to review their progress by asking themselves three questions, which I would paraphrase as follows:

1. What have I done well today with regard to self-improvement and fulfilling my potential in life?
2. Where did I go wrong in this regard?
3. What did I omit that I could do next time?

We find a different version of the same exercise in the writings of Seneca, another Stoic, who adds

> I make use of this privilege, and daily plead my cause before myself. When the lamp is taken out of my sight, and my wife, who knows my habit, has ceased to talk, I pass the whole day in review before myself, and repeat all that I have said and done. I conceal nothing from myself, and omit nothing. (*On Anger*)

However, in the most famous Stoic text of all, *The Meditations* of Marcus Aurelius, we have his own personal notebook or journal—the product of similar reflections on his own character and actions. This is the ancient forebearer, the great-grandaddy, of most subsequent self-help and psychotherapy literature. For example, in his *Autobiography*, Benjamin Franklin famously describes a little book, his reflective journal, based on what he called his "Plan for Attaining Moral Perfection." He tells us the inspiration came from reading about the exercise described above in the Greek classics.

You are holding in your hands, this very second, a book that stands in a venerable philosophical tradition, stretching back two millennia and more. The exercises upon which you're about to embark are echoes of those employed by Arrian on the battlefields of Asia Minor in his campaign against the Alani and by Emperor Marcus Aurelius as he led the Roman army deployed on the Danube frontier during the Marcomannic Wars. The leadership challenges you face today may seem quite different, but deep down, they're probably much the same and much the same capacity for careful reflection and moral or psychological self-examination will, fate willing, serve you just as well as it did them.

—Donald J. Robertson
Author of *How to Think Like a Roman Emperor: The Stoic Philosophy of Marcus Aurelius* (St. Martin's)

Acknowledgments

———⟨⟨⟨⟩⟩⟩———

We would like to thank the writers and readers who have supported *From the Green Notebook* over the years. Your support allowed us to build a platform that now serves as a go-to resource for the personal and professional development of leaders around the world.

Specifically, we would like to thank the volunteers who've invested so much of their free time into editing submissions and sharing our content. Those volunteers include Megan Jantos, Gary Klein, Dan Vigeant, Joshua Bowen, Valerie Nostrant, and Connor Collins.

We would also like to thank those who encouraged us: Steven Pressfield, Donald Robertson, Joseph McCormack, and Stu Conley.

Joe would like to thank his parents who allowed him to play with an old typewriter when he was a kid; his wife, Amanda, who has been his biggest supporter from the very beginning; and Brady and Sloane, who hung out in the home office while Dad worked on his "big project."

Cassie would like to thank her family and friends for their unwavering support and confidence;

her husband, Ryan, who reminds her to dream; and her daughters, Chloe and Cora, who make sure she laughs every day.

Cover designed by Katrina Faust and Jay Billups.

What Is *My Green Notebook*?

My Green Notebook: *"Know Thyself" Before Changing Jobs* is your notebook. It's a guided reflection developed to draw out your lessons learned and help you thrive as a leader as you take on positions of increased responsibility, regardless of your line of work. We believe that reading, writing, and reflection are the keys to self-improvement and development. This journal is your opportunity to spend a few minutes with yourself each day for a month and examine your experiences so that you can better understand your strengths and weaknesses and, more importantly, determine your opportunities for growth.

Why We Created It

W ith more than four decades of combined
military service and numerous combat
and operational deployments, we've each
held at least sixteen various leadership positions across
the military. Every time we changed leadership roles,
someone we trusted and respected reminded us to take
time during transition to reflect on our experiences
and learn from our mistakes, failures, and successes.
For both of us, it was years before we truly understood
or appreciated the benefit of taking the time to think
and write about the past or knew how to do it effectively. With our mutual observations, we assume many
of you have been given similar advice with little direc-
tion on how to actually approach reflection.

From these combined experiences and our
assumptions, the concept of *My Green Notebook*
emerged. We developed this notebook because, in
retrospect, it was the one we both needed and wanted
throughout the years as we transitioned from one job
to the next, grasping at ways to capture our mile-
stones, understand our developmental needs, and
see how our perspectives were changing over time.
Therefore, we want to help you avoid being as lost

as we were and making the same mistakes we made, going years at a time without the resources to reflect in a meaningful way.

We've both undergone various leadership assessments over the years. We found the common thread that determines the outcome of these various tests is the leader's level of self-awareness. Many leader assessments are constructed to draw out who you truly are as a leader, the key experiences that shaped you (good and bad), and those facets of your leadership style that still need the most work. These deep dives into your psyche and your personal attributes require you to introspect and make meaning of your revelations. When we found ourselves in these situations, we often wished then we had a source, like this notebook, to help us hone in on and make meaning of the answers we were looking for.

In recent years, our experiences with leadership coaches helped us put it all together: the lessons we learned about the importance of reflection, those lessons we learned in reflection, and the skills we developed to create actionable plans to continue to improve as leaders, even at our level of expertise. We realized the earlier a leader puts in the work to see themselves better and understand their strengths and weaknesses, the more prepared they are for the challenges that come with leading others. Most importantly, we learned it's never too late to start because personal growth is a lifelong journey, and we continue to see the benefits of reading, writing, and reflection in our own lives.

What Is Reflection?

R eflection is a process whereby we examine the past to learn from our actions and behaviors. It provides an opportunity to view ourselves as the subject, removed from the immediacy of the moment, and pick apart our thoughts about our previous decisions, actions, and behaviors. In an ongoing conscious transaction with the past, reflective thought involves contemplating both into the past and into the future to determine if past experiences and perceptions align with current reality and future desires. In these moments, we view our history constructively and explore unexpected choices and possibilities, enabling ourselves to learn and transform and empowering our past selves to become the future selves we desire.

Executive coach, Jennifer Porter, explains reflection in an HBR.org article entitled "Why You Should Make Time for Reflection," writing,

> Reflection gives the brain an opportunity to pause amidst the chaos, untangle, and sort through observations and expe-

riences, consider multiple inter-
pretations, and create meaning...
This meaning becomes learning.

This self-observation and criticism gives you
the power to answer questions such as "Am I getting the results I desire?" "Were the reasons for my
actions correct?" "Do I need to modify or change my
behavior?"

While many organizations are only now com-
ing around to the benefits of reflection, as Donald
Robertson points out in the Foreword, it is a practice
that humans have undertaken for as long as we have
been recording history.

Reflection Is an
Age-Old Tradition

For more than two millennia, history provides us with a record of people attempting to make meaning of their actions and understand themselves better. In the ancient western world, people made pilgrimages to the Temple of Delphi where they entered through a walkway with the words *Gnothi Seauton* or "Know Thyself" inscribed above the entrance. In the east, people studied the words of the philosopher Lao Tzu who wrote

> Knowing others is intelligence;
> Knowing yourself is true wisdom.
> Mastering others is strength;
> Mastering yourself is true power.

This age-old tradition of "knowing thyself" eventually became referred to as reflection as philosophers played with various paths to self-discovery. Some of the Stoic philosophers in the first century taught followers to reflect in the morning about their intentions for the day, while others taught people to reflect on their actions in the evening, writing,

> I will keep constant watch over
> myself and—most usefully—will
> put each day up for review. For
> this is what makes evil—that
> none of us looks back upon our
> lives. We reflect upon only that
> which we are about to do. And
> yet our plans for the future
> descend from the past.

Leaders throughout history have used reflection to work through problems and as a source of growth.

As Robertson reminds us in the Foreword, Emperor Marcus Aurelius wrote his *Meditations* while leading Roman legions on the frontiers of the Empire. Winston Churchill and General Dwight D. Eisenhower both used reflection and writing to think through some of the most difficult moments of the Second World War.

Prior to the D-Day landings in May of 1944, General Eisenhower listened as the commander for the air operation recommended to him that he cancel the airborne invasion, painting a grim picture of the weather and expected casualties from the Allied force. In his book *Crusade in Europe*, Ike wrote,

> I went to my tent alone and sat
> down to think. I realized of course
> that if I disregarded the advice of
> my technical expert on the sub-
> ject, and his predictions should

prove accurate, then I would carry to my grave the unbearable burden of a conscience justly accusing me of the stupid, blind sacrifice of thousands.

Several times over the next week, Ike took advantage of moments of solitude to think through the decision for the D-Day invasion and gain clarity by writing out his thoughts. At one point, he typed out a memo titled "Worries of a Commander," defining the risks of the operation and imagining a worst-case scenario. He recognized that in delaying the operation, the risk of discovery by the Nazis, intelligence breaches, and the drop in morale also rose. Yet he feared without the airborne component, the landings themselves were doomed. In those reflective moments, Ike gained the clarity he needed to make his decision, setting in motion a series of events that would lead to the Allied victory with three simple words on June 5, 1944, "Well, let's go."

The Benefits of Reflection

━━━━━━━━━ ⟊⟊⟊⟊⟩━◆━⟨⟊⟊⟊⟊ ━━━━━━━━━

While there are countless examples of reflection in practical use, scientists have also proven the benefits of looking at the past to inform the future. In the last thirty years, researchers found reflection to be an integral part of how adults learn. Dr. David Kolb, who is recognized as the father of the adult-learning model, found that reflection helps us make sense of our experiences and extract lessons that we then use to grow and develop. In 1984, Kolb wrote, "Learning is the process whereby knowledge is created through the transformation of experience." He observed that without the step of reflection, we're only getting a nibble of the lessons that experience can teach us.

In a 2016 study published by Harvard Business School, titled *The Role of Reflection in Individual Learning*, researchers found, "Once an individual has accumulated a certain amount of experience with a task, the benefit of accumulating additional experience is inferior to the benefit of deliberately articulating and codifying the experience accumulated in the past." In other words, if you want to take your skills to the next level, you need to reflect and write about your past experiences!

While there are many benefits to looking at the past to make meaning in the present and determine a course of action for the future, experts also suggest a danger in not doing so.

In Morgan McCall Jr.'s seminal work, *High Flyers: Developing the Next Generation of Leaders*, he looks across multiple organizations to understand why some leaders who rise to the top of the pyramid later come crashing down. He found that a lack of reflection and self-awareness plays a major role in leader derailment. Organizations inadvertently encourage overuse of existing strengths and often neglect the development of new skills and behaviors. Due to this phenomena, he observed that as leaders move into different positions, past strengths can actually turn into weaknesses if the context in which they lead changes, but they fail to change with it. He argues that one of the ways in which leaders can prevent this from happening is to reflect on the past to understand how their strengths and weaknesses *actually* contributed to their success or failure.

If you've made it this far, we hope you have committed to this thirty-day assessment with a better understanding of how reflection will benefit you as a leader. We care about your personal development and the generation of leaders who follow in your footsteps, looking for wisdom and guidance, to create their own path to excellence. Our vision is for this notebook to provide you with the opportunity and the tools to reflect, and that in doing so, you will find the answers you're looking for on your own journey to "know thyself" as a leader and as a human.

How to Use This Book

————————∕∕∕∕◗━◖∖∖∖∖————————

This notebook is a self-assessment designed to be conducted sequentially over thirty days. We divided the next twenty-nine days into subcategories. Each day, you'll read a description of the category for that day to set the stage for your reflection. You will then be presented with questions that will require you to dedicate a few moments in deep thought before you answer. Therefore, we recommend that you set aside about ten to fifteen minutes in the morning and ten to fifteen minutes in the evening to answer the daily questions.

Day 30 is your most important day as this is the point in the process where you attempt to make sense of your reflections. On this day, you will look back across your answers to identify patterns in behavior and seek deeper meaning from your revelations. You will then be asked to determine what you can stop doing, what you can start doing, and what you can sustain. You will consider the resources you require to further understand your desired outcomes and develop an actionable plan to become the leader you wish to be.

We know many of you will be tempted to sit down and slog your way through all thirty days in one setting, anxious to get to the end where the real magic occurs. While your intent may be noble, we fear you will fail to achieve the outcome you desire. We admit reflection is tough and requires a candor and honesty with yourself that may leave you feeling drained and depleted. You may find it difficult to think back on some of your experiences and realize you could have been more effective or made a better decision. Or you may be triggered by the memory of an event that, at the time, caused you to spin out of control, but in retrospect, turned out to be your ego holding you back. On the other hand, you may be energized by the validation that many of your actions and behaviors led to your success, your decisions were sound, and the relationships you enjoy truly are as whole and complete as you think they are.

Either way, we urge you to stare into the void, to hold these experiences in your hands, examine them purely and thoroughly, and gaze at them with fresh eyes. Find comfort in your discomfort and new meaning in old behaviors. These moments are yours to do with what you will, but as author Steven Pressfield reminds us in a blog post on his website,

> Deep change (in our real lives, as well as fiction) happens not in clamorous action-filled moments but in quiet, pensive beats when the human heart, at the finish of

a protracted, often unconscious,
process of evolution concludes
and cements its transformation.

Getting the most out of this experience will require some deep introspection and a commitment to savor the experiences that await you among these pages. Embrace this process and allow yourself the quiet moments to think and the silent moments to fully transform.

Our ancestors made their way to the Oracle of Delphi to not only "know thyself," but to know the future. In understanding where we have come from, we can determine where we are headed and take our next steps with intention.

D A Y 1

Setting My Intention

Day 1 sets the stage for the rest of your journey. Your intention is your "why." In this instance, your "why" drew you to this notebook in the first place and helped you see a need in yourself for this thirty-day assessment. Today, you will be asked to think about your "why" and your plan to hold yourself accountable throughout this journey. Finally, setting your intention will empower you to approach this notebook wholly, deliberately, and purposefully.

What do I hope to gain from this journey with *My Green Notebook*?

_____

_____

_____

_____

_____

_____

_____

_____

_____

_____

_____

_____

_____

_____

_____

_____

_____

_____

_____

_____

How will I hold myself accountable to get to day 30?

_____

_____

_____

_____

_____

_____

_____

_____

_____

_____

_____

_____

_____

_____

_____

_____

_____

_____

D A Y 2

Getting Results

Leaders who get results turn their vision, goals, and objectives into reality and focus on the quality of their organization's outputs rather than the quantity. Getting results means seeking meaningful outcomes and aspiring for both efficiency and effectiveness. Leaders get results when the tasks they take on, and those they delegate, align with the organization's priorities and their boss' intent. In the event of failure, those who get results react in deliberate ways and seek to learn so they are prepared when faced with similar challenges in the future.

What is something that I'm proud I accomplished in my most recent position and what factors influenced the outcome?

_____

_____

_____

_____

_____

_____

_____

_____

_____

_____

_____

_____

_____

_____

_____

_____

_____

_____

_____

_____

How did I hold others accountable? What tools were most effective in doing so?

_____

_____

_____

_____

_____

_____

_____

_____

_____

_____

_____

_____

_____

_____

_____

_____

_____

_____

_____

D A Y 3

Adaptability

daptability is required in situations for which we lack the mental models and experience to understand how to behave, act, or make decisions that lead us toward our objectives. When faced with change, adaptability allows the individual or organization to modify behavior while continuing to pursue its intended purpose. Effective adaptation requires leaders to consider the impacts of their decisions and actions on others, as well as potential second and third order effects.

What was the biggest change I faced? How did I handle it, and what did I learn from it?

_____

_____

_____

_____

_____

_____

_____

_____

_____

_____

_____

_____

_____

_____

_____

_____

_____

_____

_____

What was a change I implemented, and how did I prepare my team for change? What would I do differently if I had to do it over again?

_____

_____

_____

_____

_____

_____

_____

_____

_____

_____

_____

_____

_____

_____

_____

_____

_____

_____

D A Y 4

————⟊⟊⟊⟊⟊●⟊⟊⟊⟊———

Learning

L earning is the key to a leader's ability to innovate and adapt in a complex environment. When leaders have a learning or growth mindset, they value progress over perfection and take every opportunity as one to take on new understanding, skills, attitudes, and behaviors. They block time to make sense of their experiences and prevent failures or successes from becoming value judgments and instead, make them data points for growth.

What was the most difficult task I had to learn? How did I approach it?

_____

_____

_____

_____

_____

_____

_____

_____

_____

_____

_____

_____

_____

_____

_____

_____

_____

_____

_____

What was the most important lesson I learned about myself?

_____

_____

_____

_____

_____

_____

_____

_____

_____

_____

_____

_____

_____

_____

_____

_____

_____

_____

_____

DAY 5

———— ◦◦◦◦•••◦◦◦◦ ————

Analyzing Information

Many leaders are overloaded with information and have to make meaningful decisions, even when presented with ambiguous and incomplete data sets. Analyzing information requires leaders to gather information from multiple sources, determine which information is viable, and make sense of it in the context of their environment.

How did I determine priorities? Were there other priorities I should have considered?

_____

_____

_____

_____

_____

_____

_____

_____

_____

_____

_____

_____

_____

_____

_____

_____

_____

_____

_____

_____

When did I foresee an emerging problem? What did I do with my intuition, and how did my actions influence the outcome?

_____

_____

_____

_____

_____

_____

_____

_____

_____

_____

_____

_____

_____

_____

_____

_____

_____

_____

_____

D A Y 6

Assertiveness

Assertiveness is derived from a leader's ability to navigate between their personal boundaries and the needs, wants, and desires of others. The assertive leader speaks up for themselves and those in their charge, while maintaining humility and a calm and collected demeanor, even in the face of adversity. They address problems before they become unmanageable without becoming overly aggressive or offensive. By carefully considering the perspective of those with whom they interact, they prevent self-confidence from becoming self-importance.

What did I tolerate? What prevented me from speaking up?

_____

_____

_____

_____

_____

_____

_____

_____

_____

_____

_____

_____

_____

_____

_____

_____

_____

_____

_____

_____

When was a time I said yes to additional work or tasks when I really wanted to say no because I already had a lot on my plate? What prevented me from saying no?

_____

_____

_____

_____

_____

_____

_____

_____

_____

_____

_____

_____

_____

_____

_____

_____

_____

_____

DAY 7

————⟪⟫————

Rigor

Rigor involves the use of discipline, standards, thoroughness, consistencies, and institutional models to set the bar high for those who excel within the organization. For those who seek excellence, rigor in the system demands consistency of performance. It keeps those you lead and you challenged and engaged, both in the office and in training.

When did I overlook a major mistake, and what prevented me from catching it? How did I fix it?

_____

_____

_____

_____

_____

_____

_____

_____

_____

_____

_____

_____

_____

_____

_____

_____

_____

_____

_____

If I found an error in someone else's work, did I inform them of the error, and if so, how did I tell them? If not, what prevented me from bringing it up?

_____

_____

_____

_____

_____

_____

_____

_____

_____

_____

_____

_____

_____

_____

_____

_____

_____

_____

D A Y 8

Mentorship

Mentors help organizations and institutions grow and develop future generations of leaders. An effective mentor listens, coaches, and guides a person of lesser experience with mutual trust and respect as the foundation of that relationship. Mentors seek to understand the strengths and weaknesses of their proteges so they can tailor advice based on who they are, rather than who the mentor wants them to be, and empower them to embody their full potential.

When was the last time I asked a junior leader about their career or life aspirations? How did I respond to their desires and enable their success?

_____

_____

_____

_____

_____

_____

_____

_____

_____

_____

_____

_____

_____

_____

_____

_____

_____

_____

_____

_____

What topics did I discuss with mentees? How did I prepare for these conversations?

_____

_____

_____

_____

_____

_____

_____

_____

_____

_____

_____

_____

_____

_____

_____

_____

_____

_____

_____

_____

_____

D A Y 9

Verbal Communication

Effective communicators consider their audience, come prepared with clear and concise messages and talking points, and speak with confidence. Leaders often have to synthesize large amounts of data, distilling it to its salient parts and then using that enhanced understanding to share knowledge and influence audiences. Verbal communication is the cornerstone of gaining shared understanding and, clearly, communicating intent.

How often did my subordinates need to seek clarification or further guidance after I communicated guidance or intent?

_____

_____

_____

_____

_____

_____

_____

_____

_____

_____

_____

_____

_____

_____

_____

_____

_____

_____

_____

How did I prepare myself to speak in front of a group? What could I have done better?

_____

_____

_____

_____

_____

_____

_____

_____

_____

_____

_____

_____

_____

_____

_____

_____

_____

_____

_____

_____

D A Y   1 0

Active Listening

This type of listening requires the leader to pay attention to body language and behavior and withhold judgment and responses until the speaker finishes. The listener should seek clarification when needed and be able to summarize if asked. Effective leaders encourage candid feedback and use active listening to fully understand what someone is saying to them beyond just what they are hearing.

What do I do to ensure I'm listening actively?

_____

_____

_____

_____

_____

_____

_____

_____

_____

_____

_____

_____

_____

_____

_____

_____

_____

_____

_____

What are some distractions that prevent me from listening actively?

_____

_____

_____

_____

_____

_____

_____

_____

_____

_____

_____

_____

_____

_____

_____

_____

_____

_____

_____

DAY 11

Trust

Trust is the foundation of any relationship and the basis for organizational effectiveness. When leaders demonstrate trust, it empowers those they lead to act with purpose and confidence. Leaders earn and maintain the trust of others by remaining true to their word, treating others with dignity and respect, and modeling vulnerability and authenticity.

How did my subordinates earn my trust?

_____

_____

_____

_____

_____

_____

_____

_____

_____

_____

_____

_____

_____

_____

_____

_____

_____

_____

_____

_____

_____

Who was in my circle of trust? If there were those who remained outside my circle of trust, how did I make them feel valued?

_____

_____

_____

_____

_____

_____

_____

_____

_____

_____

_____

_____

_____

_____

_____

_____

_____

_____

_____

_____

D A Y   1 2

———⟡———

Written
Communication

The ability to communicate effectively using the written word takes time to develop, but it's worth the investment. Clear and concise writers inform, influence, and serve as a catalyst for action across organizations. Writing, like most strenuous activities, requires practice to improve efficiency, reading to enhance knowledge, and reflection to continue to learn. Once leaders hone their ability to communicate in writing, their most dangerous weapon becomes the pen.

How would I describe my comfort level with written communication? Are there areas I avoid? If so, why?

_____

_____

_____

_____

_____

_____

_____

_____

_____

_____

_____

_____

_____

_____

_____

_____

_____

_____

_____

_____

_____

What did I do to improve my written communication?

_____

_____

_____

_____

_____

_____

_____

_____

_____

_____

_____

_____

_____

_____

_____

_____

_____

_____

_____

_____

D A Y   1 3

Self-Control

Our brains run on two systems: one controlled and one automatic. Logical thinking is found in the controlled side of the brain, whereas gut feelings, emotions, and visceral reactions are found in the automatic side. Logical thinking feeds self-control, allowing leaders to maintain composure in the face of ambiguity, adversity, and conflict.

When did I become extremely angry or upset at work? What triggered me? What was the outcome?

_____

_____

_____

_____

_____

_____

_____

_____

_____

_____

_____

_____

_____

_____

_____

_____

_____

_____

_____

_____

_____

What is one habit that I found myself having to control to not create conflict in an organization (talk behind people's backs, eye rolls, cursing, etc.)? What made it most difficult to control this habit?

_____

_____

_____

_____

_____

_____

_____

_____

_____

_____

_____

_____

_____

_____

_____

_____

_____

_____

D A Y   1 4

———————— ⟨⟨⟨⟨⟨●⟩⟩⟩⟩⟩ ————————

Interpersonal Relationships

Humans are social beings, and therefore, relationships are a critical component of our existence. Properly managing the interpersonal nature of relationships is both an art and a science. Those who struggle to build and maintain relationships can improve with a better understanding of the science of human behavior and practice in the art of influence. Leaders who operate effectively in the human domain establish and respect boundaries, encourage others, actively listen, and approach difficult conversations with candor and humility.

What was an interpersonal interaction that later made me change my behavior based on the outcome?

_____

_____

_____

_____

_____

_____

_____

_____

_____

_____

_____

_____

_____

_____

_____

_____

_____

_____

_____

How did I receive feedback from others? What did I learn about myself from this feedback? If I did not receive feedback, what prevented me from doing so?

_____

_____

_____

_____

_____

_____

_____

_____

_____

_____

_____

_____

_____

_____

_____

_____

_____

_____

_____

D A Y   1 5

Managing Conflict

Conflict is rooted in human behavior, which means every relationship among individuals and teams is going to experience conflict. To mitigate the deleterious effects that can arise from conflict among stakeholders, individual team members should learn to facilitate tough conversations, provide constructive feedback as necessary, and de-escalate contentious situations in support of the goals of the organization.

Who was the most difficult person I worked with and what made them so difficult? How did I handle this person?

_____

_____

_____

_____

_____

_____

_____

_____

_____

_____

_____

_____

_____

_____

_____

_____

_____

_____

_____

How did I approach difficult conversations?

_____

_____

_____

_____

_____

_____

_____

_____

_____

_____

_____

_____

_____

_____

_____

_____

_____

_____

_____

_____

DAY 16

Self-Development

M any experiences provide individuals with opportunities for development. Self-development, however, is a deliberate focus on learning skills to succeed in life or a given profession. Leaders should take responsibility for their own development and seek out experiences that allow them to learn and challenge the limits of their capabilities. They should read, write, and reflect to better understand themselves and the potential impacts of their behavior and broaden their repertoire from which to draw meaning.

When did I fail, and what did I learn from it?

_____

_____

_____

_____

_____

_____

_____

_____

_____

_____

_____

_____

_____

_____

_____

_____

_____

_____

_____

_____

_____

What steps did I take to identify areas where I needed to improve, and how did I measure progress?

_____

_____

_____

_____

_____

_____

_____

_____

_____

_____

_____

_____

_____

_____

_____

_____

_____

_____

_____

_____

DAY 17

Innovation

To adapt to novel surroundings, one must either apply preexisting information to a new context or find novel ways to continue to excel by experimenting with alternative ways to approach the environment. Innovative leaders aspire for change, evolve to grow, and extend their new-found knowledge to the collective. They are comfortable with discomfort and approach ambiguity with curiosity and wonder.

How did I innovate to achieve a desired result?

_____

_____

_____

_____

_____

_____

_____

_____

_____

_____

_____

_____

_____

_____

_____

_____

_____

_____

_____

What activities did I pursue outside of work to expand my perspective or break away from the monotony of my daily tasks?

_____

_____

_____

_____

_____

_____

_____

_____

_____

_____

_____

_____

_____

_____

_____

_____

_____

_____

D A Y   1 8

Critical Thinking

I n today's information-rich environment, critical thinking is a necessary skill to weed through various data sets and sources of information to either reinforce or challenge one's worldview. Honing critical-thinking skills requires broadening one's perspective through education, reading, and gaining experience. The sum of that knowledge provides leaders with sound judgment to make decisions that result in organizational success.

When did I use outside resources to solve a problem?
How did I know which resources were available?

_____

_____

_____

_____

_____

_____

_____

_____

_____

_____

_____

_____

_____

_____

_____

_____

_____

_____

_____

Describe a time I failed to see the second or third order effects of my actions. What did I learn?

_____

_____

_____

_____

_____

_____

_____

_____

_____

_____

_____

_____

_____

_____

_____

_____

_____

_____

_____

_____

_____

D A Y   1 9

Decision-Making

Leaders are required to constantly assess the amount of decision space they have in relation to a particular decision, which may or may not be clearly defined. Rational decision-making requires organizing and analyzing the available data sets to inform the final judgment. When leaders hold on to decisions that require immediate action, they lose opportunities as options begin to expire. On the other hand, when they make decisions in haste that require more context, they can find themselves embroiled in a messy cleanup operation. The most effective leaders cultivate context and prioritize their decisions based on those that require immediate action and those that allow for the situation to develop.

What was the toughest decision I made? How did I weigh the factors of the decision? What was the impact?

_____

_____

_____

_____

_____

_____

_____

_____

_____

_____

_____

_____

_____

_____

_____

_____

_____

_____

_____

How do I approach important decisions, and from whom do I seek counsel, if anyone?

_____

_____

_____

_____

_____

_____

_____

_____

_____

_____

_____

_____

_____

_____

_____

_____

_____

_____

DAY 20

Developing Others

Effective leaders invest in the professional development of those they lead to optimize performance and help them attain the skills necessary to perform at levels of increased responsibility. In developing others, leaders must provide candid performance feedback and insights to leverage strengths appropriately, develop plans to improve weaknesses, and provide the resources to enable transformation.

How often did I give feedback to subordinates? What were the various types of feedback I gave? Which approaches seemed more effective than others?

_____

_____

_____

_____

_____

_____

_____

_____

_____

_____

_____

_____

_____

_____

_____

_____

_____

_____

_____

_____

How did I empower others?

_____

_____

_____

_____

_____

_____

_____

_____

_____

_____

_____

_____

_____

_____

_____

_____

_____

_____

_____

DAY 21

Self-Confidence

S elf-confidence is a belief in one's own abilities, judgment, or qualities. It is rooted in people's understanding of their strengths and weaknesses, and may or may not, reflect reality because it is based on the perspective of the self. Self-confidence is also contextual and relative to the situation, so it's common for people to have high self-confidence in one area but low self-confidence in another. Understanding where those areas lie are key to gaining insight into one's developmental needs.

What aspects of the job made me feel confident in my abilities to complete assigned tasks or perform at the level expected?

_____

_____

_____

_____

_____

_____

_____

_____

_____

_____

_____

_____

_____

_____

_____

_____

_____

_____

_____

_____

What aspects of the job made me question my abilities to complete assigned tasks or perform at the level expected?

_____

_____

_____

_____

_____

_____

_____

_____

_____

_____

_____

_____

_____

_____

_____

_____

_____

_____

_____

DAY 22

Extending Influence

Organizations are more than the function of a line and block chart on the wall. They are made up of people and the stakeholders who support them. The relationships between individuals inside and outside the organization are a key factor in that organization's success. Effective leaders build and maintain networks of influence that allow their organizations to thrive and survive, cooperating with the collective to strengthen the individual.

How did I develop and maintain relationships outside of my organization?

_____

_____

_____

_____

_____

_____

_____

_____

_____

_____

_____

_____

_____

_____

_____

_____

_____

_____

_____

_____

What task did I face that required buy-in from external stakeholders? How did I approach it?

_____

_____

_____

_____

_____

_____

_____

_____

_____

_____

_____

_____

_____

_____

_____

_____

_____

_____

_____

DAY 23

Integrity

The word integrity comes from the Latin *integritas*, meaning "wholeness." A person with integrity has all the facets of their life integrated and maintains a consistency across their words, actions, and beliefs. Authenticity and transparency are inherent in a leader's ability to allow others to perceive this consistency in behavior. Effective leaders make promises they can keep and uphold the values by which they actually live.

When did a job requirement cause me to struggle to align the decision I knew was necessary with my personal values?

_____

_____

_____

_____

_____

_____

_____

_____

_____

_____

_____

_____

_____

_____

_____

_____

_____

_____

What behaviors do I exhibit that could be construed as hypocritical if those I lead knew the "real me"?

_____

_____

_____

_____

_____

_____

_____

_____

_____

_____

_____

_____

_____

_____

_____

_____

_____

_____

_____

_____

DAY 24

⎯⎯⎯⎯⎯⎯⎯◦⎯⎯⎯⎯⎯⎯⎯

Inclusion

Humans are tribal creatures and have an innate desire for a sense of belonging. Individuals are greatly influenced by the people they surround themselves with, who they choose can either expand their perspective or reinforce their personal narrative. Leaders who are mindful of the people they rely on for advice can ensure those who work for them feel valued, and they receive input from multiple and varied perspectives.

What kinds of people do I surround myself with?

_____

_____

_____

_____

_____

_____

_____

_____

_____

_____

_____

_____

_____

_____

_____

_____

_____

_____

_____

_____

_____

What kinds of people do I find it difficult to develop relationships with?

_____

_____

_____

_____

_____

_____

_____

_____

_____

_____

_____

_____

_____

_____

_____

_____

_____

_____

_____

_____

DAY 25

——⊸⊷——

Agility

Agility is the ability to rapidly adjust to changing events and circumstances, building new intellectual pathways, and synthesizing large amounts of information in a short amount of time. Agile leaders recognize the interplay between the mind, the body, and the environment in one's ability to make meaning. They set conditions to enable others to think and allow effective problem-solving to occur naturally.

What was an unfamiliar problem I faced? How did I make sense of it to reach a solution?

_____

_____

_____

_____

_____

_____

_____

_____

_____

_____

_____

_____

_____

_____

_____

_____

_____

_____

_____

_____

How did I optimize the environment for problem-solving?

_____

_____

_____

_____

_____

_____

_____

_____

_____

_____

_____

_____

_____

_____

_____

_____

_____

_____

_____

DAY 26

Risk-Taking

Every decision in life in which the outcome is uncertain involves some level of risk. However, progress can only occur when someone is willing to deviate from a known point or a comfortable position. Every leader has a different level of risk tolerance. If tolerance is too low, a leader may battle with anxiety and indecision and place too many controls over a situation, stifling initiative. If tolerance is too high, a leader may take rash risks, resulting in unnecessary loss of capital or even life. Leaders must continually weigh potential futures when making decisions and manage the constant tension between probability and severity of outcome.

What was the biggest risk I took? How did I go about making that decision? What was the result?

_____

_____

_____

_____

_____

_____

_____

_____

_____

_____

_____

_____

_____

_____

_____

_____

_____

_____

_____

What risk(s) did I refuse to take, and why?

_____

_____

_____

_____

_____

_____

_____

_____

_____

_____

_____

_____

_____

_____

_____

_____

_____

_____

_____

_____

DAY 27

Teamwork

Teams are the ultimate tool for organizational effectiveness. Disparate multifunctional teams can overcome any obstacle to accomplish complex tasks...if they can just work to work together effectively. In a healthy environment, teams and teammates cooperate rather than compete, understanding that individuals are stronger in the collective.

How often and under what circumstances did I offer assistance to my peers?

_____

_____

_____

_____

_____

_____

_____

_____

_____

_____

_____

_____

_____

_____

_____

_____

_____

_____

_____

_____

How did I ensure my team understood their mission? How often did I have to reiterate our purpose or objectives to keep them on track?

_____

_____

_____

_____

_____

_____

_____

_____

_____

_____

_____

_____

_____

_____

_____

_____

_____

_____

_____

DAY 28

————〰〰━〰〰————

Work/Life Tension

The search to achieve a perfect balance between work, family, and focus on the self is an endless endeavor. Life's responsibilities present a constant tension between the things people want to do in search of fulfillment and the things they need to do to survive. Balance even further relies on an individual's weighting of the importance of wants versus needs.

How did I make time for the most important personal tasks or family requirements?

_____

_____

_____

_____

_____

_____

_____

_____

_____

_____

_____

_____

_____

_____

_____

_____

_____

_____

_____

_____

_____

What work task or requirement took up the most of my time?

_____

_____

_____

_____

_____

_____

_____

_____

_____

_____

_____

_____

_____

_____

_____

_____

_____

_____

_____

_____

DAY 29

———∞∞——

Purpose

Understanding your purpose helps you find meaning in life, define your interests, and determine where you want to contribute. This part of the assessment may be the most difficult as it requires deep introspection of not just the areas in life you are good at, but also those that bring you joy.

When was a time I performed at my best? What factors of that situation allowed me to excel, and how did I feel in those moments?

_____

_____

_____

_____

_____

_____

_____

_____

_____

_____

_____

_____

_____

_____

_____

_____

_____

_____

_____

What is the next step in my career, and how does it align with my long-term goals?

_____

_____

_____

_____

_____

_____

_____

_____

_____

_____

_____

_____

_____

_____

_____

_____

_____

_____

_____

_____

D A Y 3 0

—————⟨⟨⟨⟩⟩⟩—————

My Final Assessment

ongratulations! You made it to day 30. Now we want you to take a few moments to skim back through the pages of this notebook and attempt to find meaning in your own words. Today, you will synthesize the lessons of your reflections to develop some actionable steps to become an even better leader and hold yourself accountable for the outcomes you desire. Frame your answers to today's questions around changes you are actually willing to make. Today is not about what should happen, but about what can happen with your courage and commitment.

What should I continue doing?

_____

_____

_____

_____

_____

_____

_____

_____

_____

_____

_____

_____

_____

_____

_____

_____

_____

_____

_____

_____

_____

What should I stop doing?

_____

_____

_____

_____

_____

_____

_____

_____

_____

_____

_____

_____

_____

_____

_____

_____

_____

_____

_____

What should I start doing?

_____

_____

_____

_____

_____

_____

_____

_____

_____

_____

_____

_____

_____

_____

_____

_____

_____

_____

_____

_____

What resources do I need?

_____

_____

_____

_____

_____

_____

_____

_____

_____

_____

_____

_____

_____

_____

_____

_____

_____

_____

_____

_____

How will I hold myself accountable?

_____

_____

_____

_____

_____

_____

_____

_____

_____

_____

_____

_____

_____

_____

_____

_____

_____

_____

_____

_____

_____

Selected Bibliography

Dweck, Carol. *Mindset: The New Psychology of Success*. New York: Random House, 2016.

Di Stefano, Giada and Gino, Francesca and Pisano, Gary and Staats, Bradley R. *Making Experience Count: The Role of Reflection in Individual Learning* (June 14, 2016). Harvard Business School NOM Unit Working Paper No. 14-093, Harvard Business School Technology & Operations Mgt. Unit Working Paper No. 14-093, HEC Paris Research Paper No. SPE-2016-1181, Available at SSRN: https://ssrn.com/abstract=2414478 or http://dx.doi.org/10.2139/ssrn.2414478.

Eisenhower, Susan. *How Ike Led: The Principles Behind Eisenhower's Biggest Decisions*. St. Martin's Publishing Group, 2020.

Eisenhower, Dwight. *Crusade in Europe*. Doubleday, 1952.

Hays, Gregory. *Meditations: A New Translation*. Modern Library, 2003.

Haidt, Jonathan. *The Happiness Hypothesis: Finding Modern Truth in Ancient Wisdom*. Basic Books, 2006.

Kimball, Ray. *The Army Officer's Guide to Mentoring*. Center for the Advancement of Leader Development and Organizational Learning, 2019.

Peterson, C., and Seligman, M. E. P. *Character strengths and virtues: A handbook and classification*. Oxford University Press: American Psychological Association, 2004.

Porter, Jennifer. *Why You Should Make Time for Self-Reflection (Even If You Hate Doing It)*. Harvard Business Review: https://hbr.org/2017/03/why-you-should-make-time-for-self-reflection-even-if-you-hate-doing-it, 2014.

Pressfield, Steve. *The Power of a Private Moment*. www.stevenpressfield.com. https://stevenpressfield.com/2021/02/the-power-of-a-private-moment/, 2021.

Robertson, Donald. *How to Think Like a Roman Emperor: The Stoic Philosophy of Marcus Aurelius*. St Martin's Publishing Group, 2019.

What Are You Reading Next?

For more resources, check out www.from-thegreennotebook.com.

- Each week, the site publishes new articles based on leadership lessons learned written by military leaders from all over the world.
- Download the latest episodes of the *From the Green Notebook Podcast*, where the team dives into the notebooks of military leaders, business professionals, authors, athletes, coaches, and entertainers to examine lessons that will help listeners lead with the best version of themselves.
- Join thousands of others and subscribe to the "Monthly Reading List Email" to learn about new books for your personal and professional growth.
- Subscribe to the "Sunday Email" for weekly quotes and passages to make you reflect on the type of leader you want to become.

About the Authors

Joe is an active-duty army officer and the founder of *From the Green Notebook*. He's a graduate of the University of North Georgia and Naval War College. Over the years, Joe's been a contributing writer to multiple professional journals and magazines and a contributing author to two books. He's also a non-resident fellow at the Modern War Institute.

Cassie is a leadership coach with extensive experience leading multifunctional teams in dynamic and complex environments. She has a BA in English from University of New Hampshire, an MBA in Organizational Leadership from Norwich University, and a master of Military Art and Science in Operational Planning from the US Army School of Advanced Military Studies. She is the founder and principal of Iterata Solutions, a leadership coaching and consulting company.

Printed in the USA
CPSIA information can be obtained
at www.ICGtesting.com
LVHW021806041023
760085LV00005B/42

9 781638 600855